Controlling the Costs of Employee Benefits

edited by Theresa Brothers

Contents

From the President

Employee benefits managers are facing a growing number of questions about benefit plans. Employees, retirees and senior executives alike are concerned about spiraling costs as well as increasingly complex features of health care and pension fund contributions.

At the Board's 1992 Employee Benefits Conference, executives discussed new ways to maintain competitive benefits for the recruitment and retention of qualified workers, while easing the burden on their corporations. This report highlights their experiences.

The Conference Board is grateful to the conference participants and to those who contributed their insights to this report.

PRESTON TOWNLEY
President and CEO

Executive Summary

The employee benefits dilemma of the 1990s can be briefly summed up: Many employers can no longer afford to maintain the high level of benefits to which employees have become accustomed. However, employers cannot afford not to have competitive benefits to recruit and retain skilled, highly motivated employees. How companies are walking this tightrope was the topic of the 1992 Employee Benefits Conference.

According to Gallup surveys conducted for the Employee Benefit Research Institute, nearly three-quarters of U.S. workers say employee benefits are crucial to job choice. But the rising cost for medical care (for both active workers and retirees) and the increasing pressure on pension funds are causing more companies to rethink their benefit packages.

Problems With Pension Funds

Due to expected deficits from underfunded pension plans, the Bush Administration has proposed some structural changes to the Pension Benefit Guaranty Corporation (PBGC), which insures defined benefit plans. For example, companies may be seeing changes in PBGC's minimum funding rules. In addition, PBGC may apply more pressure to companies to fully fund their pension plans by only guaranteeing increases to fully funded plans.

Some companies are looking at ways to improve their current pension plans. Buck Consultants, for example, has developed a simple retirement fund which mixes the best of defined benefit and defined contribution plans. Bank of America has modified its pension plan to provide portability and simplicity and to motivate younger workers to begin their retirement savings early.

Restructuring Medical Benefits

The skyrocketing cost of health care has become a major concern of benefits managers as both senior executive and employee dissatisfaction has grown. Joseph Martingale of Towers, Perrin, Forster & Crosby discusses how medical plans have evolved since the 1970s, ushering in the current era of managed care. Charlene Rothkopf of Marriott Corporation and Kathleen O. Angel of Digital Equipment Corporation discuss their companies' experiences with this relatively new concept in health care.

Company concern with ensuring quality and cost effectiveness has also grown. For example, FMC Corporation has recently begun to track the performance of its medical plan administration, a critical factor in employee satisfaction, and has set high standards for its medical plan administrator. Jack E. Bruner of Hewitt Associates suggests a total quality approach to measurement: A company should focus on those variables it can affect; conduct audits with the purpose of improving the system; and measure results over a period of time, not just once. Ron Z. Goetzel of Johnson & Johnson Health Management, Inc. warns, however, that program evaluation is complicated by factors that need to be taken into account before drawing conclusions.

Another growing concern of employers is the aging population and the health care employees will need in retirement. Retirees are particularly worried about health care, as advancing years mean higher health care costs and a greater portion of income spent on health care coverage. According to Peter J. Dowd from Ernst & Young, companies may find retirees willing to pay high contributions to keep the security of health insurance.

Robert W. Sears of Coopers & Lybrand notes that the fastest growing segment of the U.S. population is the 80-and-older group—about 15 percent of people over age 65 will spend more than $80,000 for long term care. Some companies are already offering long term care insurance, and more are expected to do so in the future, partly as a result of the movement toward placing responsibility for retirement planning squarely on employees.

General Electric Company and International Business Machines Corporation instituted long term care plans as their employees recognized the need for such insurance. An executive from each company discusses how each plan was established, its components, and employees' and retirees' responses.

The Changing Role of the Benefits Manager

A number of business leaders discuss the skills which benefits managers will need in the coming decade. Executives from Citibank, N.A., PepsiCo Incorporated, and IBM generally agree that benefits managers will need to be more flexible, work more closely with other departments, and develop communications and strategic thinking capabilities.

John Moynahan of Metropolitan Life Insurance Company also foresees changes for health care administrators. Collaboration among insurance carriers and the provider communities has already begun, but improvements in electronic technology will bring these groups still closer together.

Introduction: The Value of Benefits

Dallas L. Salisbury
President
Employee Benefit Research Institute *

One of the Institute's projects is a monthly survey conducted with Gallup. For the past four years, we have regularly asked what value employees place on benefits and what role they play in job choice. Currently, over 74 percent of all the workers in America say that employee benefits are crucial to job choice. If limited to only one benefit (beyond cash), 64 percent say to give them just health care; 14 percent ask for a pension, but that 14 percent is primarily over age 55. When limited to two benefits, 34 percent would add pension to health care, but a growing percentage ask for additional health benefits.

These survey results may seem strange until you reflect on the difference in employee satisfaction from the 1980s to the 1990s. Since the value of benefit programs has decreased while employee contributions have increased, worker satisfaction has seen a significant decline. In 1980, 86 percent of employees were satisfied with their benefits; this declined to 42 percent in 1990. Among individuals asked how their organizations' benefit programs fit their needs, 83 percent responded positively in 1980, down to 50 percent in 1990. Also, fewer employees understand the benefit programs provided (82 percent in 1980 down to 50 percent in 1990), and fewer feel their benefits are as good as those at other companies (82 percent in 1980, 42 percent in 1990).

How is overall employee morale? In 1980, 63 percent of people felt good about what they were doing and about their work environment, down to 44 percent in 1990. What do these findings show? As we have modified programs, in no way have we reduced the importance that individuals place on benefits. However, we have clearly affected both the general level of satisfaction and the general level of understanding as we have introduced complexity.

* Copyright © 1992 by Employee Benefit Research Institute. All rights reserved.

Still More Change to Come

The demographic shifts since the 1980s are mild compared to what lies ahead. In both 1980 and 1990, 12 percent of the population was over age 65. By the year 2000, another 5 million individuals will bring the over-age-65 group to 13 percent of total population; this will be the first significant percentage increase of the last 20 years. However, life expectancy has also increased— from age 73 in 1980 to age 75 in 1989. Those numbers, however, can be extraordinarily misleading to individuals for retirement planning purposes; for some groups, life expectancy is closer to 83.

If we think about what that means for those in the benefits finance business, we find rising annuity costs, rising retiree medical costs, increasing pressures on organizations to compete with others in employing younger workers, having fewer retirees on the continuing rolls, and severing relationships that were once held sacred. Those organizations financing programs of pensions and retiree medical will find themselves under increasing pressure.

Small Business Employment on the Rise

Between 1980 and 1990, employment in businesses of fewer than 20 employees grew from 19 million to 23 million; in businesses with 20 to 29 employees, employment grew from 21 million to 25 million. Yet the 1980s actually saw the work force of employers with more than 1,000 workers drop from 10.7 million (14 percent of all workers) in 1980 to 10.65 million (12 percent of all workers) in 1990. Demographics suggest that by the year 2000 that figure will be below 10 percent. In addition to this trend, full- and part-time employment is down.

What do these statistics mean for employee benefits and employee benefit finance? It means more individuals are working for companies or in jobs where, as a matter of tradition, employee benefits have not been provided. This movement is already visible: In 1980, of all workers in America, 45 percent had pension coverage; by 1990, that number had declined to 42 percent, and we can expect it to fall to about 37 percent by the year 2000. Of full-time workers in 1990, 50 percent had pension participation; among part-time and contingent workers in 1990, only 11 percent had any form of pension participation. This trend underscores the growing importance of Social Security as well as individual efforts in savings.

Pensions vs. Health Care

Although individuals disagree on the method, business and political leaders consistently communicate the message that all Americans are entitled to health care. In actuality, only 56 percent of all workers had private health insurance protection in 1990; that figure will decline to about 50 percent by the year 2000 if nothing changes. In 1990, of full-time workers in the private sector, 67.4 percent had health insurance; only 15 percent of part-timers had it. In companies with under 25 employees, the figure was only 17 percent.

Clearly, the shift of employees to small businesses or spin-offs with little or no health coverage, in addition to fewer individuals able to purchase health insurance outside the employment setting, has led to pressure for change, for government action. Since corporate and political leaders agree that people are entitled to health care, that pressure will intensify.

During the 1980s, companies responded to the plea for health coverage by cutting by more than half the amount of money being contributed to pension programs while doubling the amount being spent on health care as a percentage of compensation (see chart). As a result of growing stock markets, good investment returns, and the ability of corporations to continue on the short side of allocation of dollars to the pension system, this trend should continue at least to 1994. But what will happen when American corporations must suddenly think about making significant contributions to their defined benefit pension programs? Where will they find the money to do it? They certainly will not be able to shift money from health care to pensions as effectively as they shifted it from pensions to health care during the 1980s. That may be the point when a massive change takes place in pension designs of companies with above 1,000 workers.

In 1980, private sector companies' total contributions to pension and profit sharing plans was $55.3 billion. By 1990, total contributions had dropped to $52.5 billion. The 1990 figure translated into 1980 dollars shows a decline of over $25 billion, or nearly 50 percent. What happened in health benefits? In 1980,

private employers spent $73 billion in health care; $209 billion in 1990. Based on current trends, which we can expect to continue, the health care number will have grown to just over $300 billion by the year 2000 while private retirement expenditures will be under $50 billion. As a percent of total compensation, in 1980 America's private businesses spent 3.4 percent of compensation on pension and profit sharing; by 1990 that had declined to 1.6 percent of compensation. During that same period, the amount spent on group health insurance went from 3.7 to 5.3 percent of compensation.

Given the reallocation of funds from pensions to health care, the question of when people will be able to afford to retire will become more important. A retirement planning benefit and life savings planning will also grow in importance. Younger employees must understand why they should start saving now and why they should not spend the lump-sum distribution but rather roll it over. If the benefit programs which began to bud in the 1980s do not increase significantly during the 1990s and beyond, then we could find ourselves back where we were decades ago, asking, "How do we get employees to retire when they are no longer economically fixed to do so?"

The Changing Make up of Medical Plans

Health plans underwent dramatic restructuring during the 1980s. Now, more companies are moving toward managed care: health maintenance organizations, preferred provider organizations, and other plans. There was a dramatic change during that period in the number of days and the circumstances covered. The addition of some benefits (such as extended care facilities) has grown significantly from 58 percent in 1980 to over 80 percent in 1990, but there has been very little change in prescription drug, diagnostics, and private-duty nursing or mental health provisions. Dental benefits grew from only 56 percent of workers in large and medium firms to 66 percent in 1990. Vision care went from 21 percent in 1980 to 35 percent in 1990.

In design and cost sharing, the 1980s also saw significant change. In 1980, only 3 percent of group health plans had deductibles of more than $150; by 1990 it was 37 percent. Co-insurance grew dramatically: While only 55 percent of plans in 1980 had any form of co-insurance, 97 percent of plans had this feature by 1990. Twenty percent of plans now have a stop loss provision, and 44 percent now require pre-admission hospital certification. We are starting to see other changes (second surgical option, non-emergency weekend admission, higher rates of payment on generic drugs, higher rates of payment on mail-order drugs), but it is really only the beginning. Flexible benefits, available to 24 percent of workers in firms with over 100 employees, is only chosen by 12 percent of those offered the opportunity.

Saving for the Future

In the most recent data point of 1990, individual retirement accounts (IRAs) had nearly $600 billion in assets compared with less than $100 billion in 1980. Although fewer individuals are contributing to IRAs since they reached their peak in 1986, the asset rate of growth in IRAs is faster than in any other pension or defined contribution arrangement because IRAs are becoming the home of lump-sum distribution roll-overs.

So we are seeing other shifts:

- Assets in defined benefit plans—$370 billion in 1980, $1.5 trillion in 1990;

- defined contribution—$106 billion in 1980, $430 billion in 1990; and

- 401(k) plans—zero in 1980, over $300 billion in 1990.

By the turn of the century, 401(k) plans are likely to pass the $500 billion mark; all defined contribution plans are likely to surpass $1 trillion; defined benefit plans are likely to stay relatively constant. Individual retirement accounts are likely to more than double in total asset value since lump-sum distributions are becoming prevalent, and these are rolled over into IRAs. All told, we are seeing substantial growth in employer-sponsored retirement programs, and based on our projections and those of the government, over 70 percent of new retirees by the year 2000 will retire with some assets that are attributable to participation in an employer-sponsored retirement program.

As a primary result of tighter vesting standards, a movement to defined contribution, and a movement to lump-sum distributions, the system is guaranteeing more and more individuals income supplementation for their retirement. However, as we move to a more small-business-dominated economy, can those trend lines be maintained? Only if small business starts to provide or help pay for health benefits, pensions and capital accumulation programs.

Securing the Pension Promise

James B. Lockhart
Executive Director
Pension Benefit Guaranty Corporation

We all benefit from a thriving economy: When companies thrive, so do their defined benefit plans, which Pension Benefit Guaranty Corporation (PBGC) insures. Because of the booming markets over the last decade, the overall pension system is extremely healthy. About $1.3 trillion is backing up $900 billion in liabilities for 40 million Americans.

Why Worry?

Indeed, the vast majority of pension plans are well funded, but there are underfunded pension plans that pose a risk to workers, retirees, and the pension insurance fund. As premium payers, your companies also face the risk of underfunded pensions and should share our concerns as the problems continue to grow. We estimate total underfunding at about $40 billion, close to a 25 percent increase from 1991. Of that total, about $13 billion are in plans where the sponsoring company is in financial trouble (a 75 percent increase from 1991). Despite aggressive efforts on our part to prevent losses, we are increasingly vulnerable to large and growing claims from underfunded pensions.

Weaknesses of particular companies and industries with large, underfunded plans have led to increased losses for us. First, we were hit with losses approaching $2 billion when the steel industry restructured. Airlines came next: Losses accrued from Pan Am and Eastern alone totaled $1.5 billion, and it is not over yet. Our annual report shows that losses for 1991 from underfunded pension plans total more than $1 billion. With these losses, the negative net worth of PBGC rose to $2.5 billion. That is more than double the deficit of only two years ago.

We are keeping our head above water with ever-escalating premiums. With the 1990 premium increase, our premium receipts continue to exceed the amount of benefits paid to retirees of the more than 1,650 plans that we have trusteed in our 17-year existence. However, this positive cash flow is expected to change as we take over more plans and as more participants in the already trusteed plans retire. Because of this long-term obligation, we are already faced with a multibillion dollar deficit. That deficit is not taking into account future claims on the insurance fund, claims that we estimate on a present value basis to be $30 billion to $45 billion. The best way to protect workers and our premium payers is to eliminate the conditions that encourage underfunded pension plans.

One reason so many people refuse to accept the fact that PBGC has a large risk is that our real financial condition is hidden; current budget accounting practices do not recognize even our known losses, let alone our expected losses. The deficits I referred to earlier are not reflected in the government budget. In fact, we actually report a surplus in the government budget at the present time of over $500 million.

Letting in the Light

President Bush's budget, introduced in January, recognized the need for reforms of the PBGC, not only to strengthen the pension safety net but also to hold up to public view our true financial position. To this end, the Bush Administration has proposed four major changes:

A shift in the federal budget treatment of insurance programs from cash accounting, which records only the yearly cash flows, to an accrual basis showing the potential long-term losses of the agency.

A clarification of our position in bankruptcy, which would reduce our losses and make sure creditors pay more attention to pension underfunding. Specifically, we want to make it clear that bankrupt companies have to make payments to ongoing plans as administrative expenses. If a plan is terminated, we want to make it clear that we have a priority for any missed contributions plus a priority for a portion of the underfunding in the plan. We also propose to gradually phase in an increase in our underfunding claim over a 20-year period, giving lenders and sponsors plenty of time to adjust to the new rules.

In addition to giving PBGC the option of becoming a member of the creditors' committee in bankruptcy proceedings, the proposals seek a priority claim for shutdown benefits that arise within three years of termination. These shutdown benefits tend to be in unionized plans and occur when a factory is shut down. That often happens right before a plan terminates. Unfortunately, these benefits are not prefunded and historically have cost us over $500 million dollars. If we get these priorities, we will have meaningful recoveries, which cause lenders to put pressure on companies to keep pension funds better funded. In bankruptcy, creditors may not be so willing to push for pension terminations when it is clear that pensions have some priority.

A tightening of minimum funding rules to speed up the funding process: The minimum funding rules enacted in 1974 and modified in 1987 have proved inadequate. In light of actual experience, the amortization rules, typically 30 years for plan amendments, though reasonable for well-funded or slightly underfunded plans, are not reducing our risk from seriously underfunded plans. The changes would not be effective until 1994, and transition rules and caps would prevent undue burden on companies. Obviously, we do not want to risk forcing companies into bankruptcy by tightening the requirements too much.

A call for PBGC to guarantee future benefit increases only in plans that are fully funded: This proposal would apply to new plan amendments. Once a plan is fully funded, all previous increases would be guaranteed.

The bulk of recent increases in pension underfunding is due to negotiated benefit increases, especially among the 50 companies with the largest underfunded plans. Because benefits are often increased at intervals as part of union negotiations, new liabilities are added before the plan gets funded up. This has led to an ever-increasing wedge of underfunding. As a result, negotiated plans are funded on average at about 75 percent while final salary plans are funded at 145 percent. Too often, the current law allows too many years to fund these new liabilities, leaving PBGC—and workers—holding a bag of empty promises.

A Solid, Equitable System

PBGC (and especially the defined benefit system), however, is far from falling apart. The defined benefit pension is still the pension of choice for most American workers because it offers a secure, guaranteed pension not subject to investment risk. But there are serious problems that must be addressed, and they lie in our very foundation. PBGC was not built on sound insurance principles. Over the years, the many attempts to patch up that foundation have just not worked. Some fundamental changes are needed now.

The cumulative effect of the Administration's proposed reforms over the years would be to create a sound insurance program based on sound insurance principles. The alternative is to drastically increase our premiums. We would need to triple the premium right now in order to cover the existing deficit and expected future claims. The vast majority of our premium payers are already paying more than their fair share. Why should our reliable sponsors foot the bill for a few others who are playing fast and loose with their pension plans?

The Administration proposals will provide the incentives necessary for companies and their creditors to take pension funding seriously. They will create a new, stronger foundation for PBGC and the pension safety net upon which 40 million American workers depend for their retirement security.

Beyond Defined Contribution or Defined Benefit Pension Plans

Vincent M. Tobin
Group Executive and Consulting Actuary
Buck Consultants

Considering all the administrative difficulties and costs involved in qualified retirement plans, why do companies have them? Contributions going into the plan are not currently charged as taxable income to the individual, and investment earnings are accumulated in the plan tax-free. At termination of employment, all moneys generated by employer contributions can be rolled over into an IRA. If not for tax-preferred treatment, it would be more efficient to simply put the value of the plan into employees' paychecks and let them do their own investing.

In order to receive tax-preferred treatment, a plan must qualify under certain Internal Revenue Code rules. Basically, the IRS considers only two types of plans: defined contribution and defined benefit. Hybrids fall somewhere in between the two.

Defined Contribution vs. Defined Benefit

Defined benefit (DB) plans may be based on average final salary, earnings over an employee's total career, or a pattern type plan which provides, say, $20 per month per year of service. Under a DB plan, the employer makes contributions to the plan which are held in a trust fund. The trust is invested and provides the benefit. If there are insufficient funds in the trust to provide benefits, PBGC insures practically all accrued pensions so that an employee has total security.

Defined contribution (DC) plans include 401(k), profit sharing, savings and thrift plans. Under a DC plan, the employee makes investment decisions and has no PBGC security on his or her account. Since employees are responsible, they will typically invest very safely. Employers usually end up putting more money into DC plans to provide a similar level of benefits because there is less appreciation on assets than in DB plans. (In a DB plan, the employer can use the upside appreciation on the assets to produce more benefits.)

If the employer is losing the upside potential, why get involved in DC plans? Financial people love them because they can be predictable if based on some percentage of compensation or matching employee contributions and affordable if based on profits. Employees love them because they get to see how much they put in, how much they earned, and their total current balance on a monthly, quarterly or yearly statement.

Defined contribution plans are also popular because problems exist with DB plans. From the employee perspective, the multiple formulas used in mature DB plans are very difficult, if not impossible, to understand. The value of the plan is obscure. If there is anything harder for the employee to understand than the Social Security offset, it is the early retirement penalty. Furthermore, from the employer point of view, high administrative costs are associated with DB plans.

Retirement Accounts Made Simple

The Cash Balance Plan is one of the most popular hybrid plans in the past seven years, and that popularity is growing. In early 1991, Buck consultants developed a type of Cash Balance Plan, called the Retirement Bonus Plan, which resembles what is known overseas as a "termination indemnity."

The most outstanding feature of the Retirement Bonus Plan is its simplicity: An employee accumulates credits until retirement; the retirement benefit is based on the number of credits multiplied by average final salary, regardless of age. For example, if the plan were designed to provide 10 credits per year and the employee retires with 30 years of service, he or she will receive a lump sum equal to 300 percent of average final salary.

In a 1991 newsletter, we described it as being like a traditional pension plan except it can be understood and appreciated. It is certainly similar to a DC plan, but instead of the account balance growing by either the actual return on investment or, as in the case of a Cash Balance Plan, with some stated rate of interest, it actually grows with the individual's own increases in pay. This can be neatly described in an employee benefits statement. Unlike a Cash Balance Plan or any DC plan, benefits from the Retirement Bonus Plan are related to average final salary, not career earnings.

Another key point of the Retirement Bonus Plan is that it provides either a pension or a lump sum. One attribute of the Cash Balance Plan is to afford the same percentage contribution for all ages and pay levels. Cash Balance Plans, therefore, supply relatively high replacement ratios for slower-track employees and relatively low replacement ratios for faster-track employees.

The Retirement Bonus, unlike defined contribution or Cash Balance, is flexible in the treatment of early terminations. Variations on the basic concept include basing the number of credits on employee age or length of service. It can be integrated with Social Security, in which case we would suggest using a step-up approach with "covered compensations" as the base.

Administrative advantages also exist. The Retirement Bonus Plan avoids the detailed record-keeping necessary for a DC plan. While we can have statements of account, we do not think they would be necessary— even annually. In addition, there is no need to credit interest each month or quarter. Finally, investment options and fund transfers are averted because the employer is controlling the assets, not the employee.

Each plan's sponsor will have individual goals. The sponsor can decide what the goals should be only after figuring out its needs and those of its employees. There must be a balance: surplus potential versus predictability of costs; an average final pay basis versus providing same cost for all; the lump sum only or pension alternative; and so on. No single solution will address every employer's problems; plenty of research, discussion with employees, and management buy-in are necessary before a decision can be made.

Pension Plan Modifications

Norman W. Snell

Senior Vice President
Bank of America

In 1985 we had about 80,000 employees, and the business was losing $600 million a year. We needed to cauterize the "bleeding" through innovation and utilization of cost savings opportunities. The company was basically fighting for its life, and the future did not look bright. To compound that problem, we are now presented with a new challenge: a merger with Security Pacific Corporation, bringing 30,000 employees into our cash balance retirement and 401(k) programs.

Like many companies in 1985, we maintained a traditional final average pay plan. It was a fairly common 2 percent per year of service plan with a typical final average base salary of five years, Social Security integration, and things of that nature. We had a 401(k) plan with a 50 percent match, which was fairly competitive at that time; however, a relatively long three years of service was required for eligibility. There was 100 percent vesting in all benefits at the time of participation. Company contributions were invested in stock only.

Weaknesses of the Old Plan

We did not want to terminate the plan because of the underfunding situation. We had an aging population and very low employee turnover. As we looked forward, we saw about 5,000 employees becoming eligible to retire over the next five years.

Under the defined benefit plan, there was a disproportionate benefit accrual to older, short-service employees versus younger, long-service ones. In a final average defined benefit plan, the younger employee probably accrues at about 1 percent of payroll versus the older, short-service accrual of 7 or 8 percent.

The pension benefit had the highest financial value at the earliest retirement age. That is, once employees reached age 55, they saw an opportunity to exit the organization and to accrue benefits elsewhere. The link between benefits and performance was weak since the final average pay formula was focused at career-end instead of performance over time. Very often, employees were confused about the plan and were continually asking questions. Several parts of the plan were both complex and difficult to understand, including Social Security supplements and pension service accounting rules. The plan was also costly to administer; every time an employee asked about his or her retirement amount, we had to tailor an individualized calculation for that employee. Record-keeping was a major issue.

Our New Strategy

In designing a new retirement plan, we first established certain objectives (see box, below). The new

---

Bank of America:
Objectives of the Cash Balance Plan

- Integrate retirement savings into total compensation.
- Institute cost control yet insure an adequate final pay replacement.
- Make the plan simple and easy to understand.
- Get employees to value the plan: We send out quarterly statements to employees so they can see their accounts building up over time.
- Acquire flexibility to be able to change the benefit formula at any point in time and not have to worry about difficulty in communicating the change.
- Offer portability so employees are able to walk away with the cash balance represented so there is distribution at any age.
- Assure age neutrality to make sure there are no unusual incentives to leave too early or late.
- Increase participation in the 401(k) plan so employees see their retirement programs as both the defined benefit and the defined contribution plans.

---

plan was called a Cash Balance Plan; it started as an individual account set up for each employee, with increases based on pay-based credits. The credits represent 4 percent of an employee's base earnings, less a Social Security wage-based offset, for employees with less than 10 years of service and 5 percent for employees with more than 10 years of service. The account balance earns interest, which is credited monthly. The interest rate is a factor based on a short-term treasury bill index and is changed annually. Our vesting changed from a 10-year cliff to a 7-year graded vesting. The distribution in our old plan was annuity based; we introduced a new option of a single lump-sum approach. We also introduced an inflation-adjusted annuity where employees have the opportunity to choose between two inflation-oriented annuities.

We also modified the 401(k) plan. Employees are now eligible after one year with the company. We increased company match contributions to 4 percent for employees with less than 10 years and 5 percent for those with more than 10 years. Also, company contributions may go into whatever fund an employee chooses within five options. In addition to a cash-out option, we introduced an annuity option for employees eligible to retire.

As part of our conversion approach, we included a five-year transition provision. In 1985, whoever retired before July 1990 would receive the higher of the Cash Balance or the old plan. Plus, we established a transitional account which minimized the reduction in the benefit for people who had long-service and/or were older employees. That meant that some employees near retirement received windfalls of 2 or 3 percent over what they would have gotten.

If We Could Do It Over...

If we had a chance to revisit the cash balance approach, we would certainly keep the portability, the vesting, the visibility and the simplicity. Those were well-received by our employees. However, we would conduct employee communications differently. With our very limited resources, we did not have an opportunity to do one-on-ones or employee meetings to the extent we would have liked. We were basically limited to some written communications and videos. A few concepts we now subscribe to:

- Do not oversell the program;

- be honest and truthful with employees;

- make sure communication is easy to understand and friendly; and

- most important, provide tools that allow employees to carry out "what if" scenarios.

401(k) plans in particular need to be constantly communicated. Do not expect lower-paid, younger employees to voluntarily enroll in them. About every quarter, we focus on those employees who do not participate in the plan and try to get them involved because it is an integral part of the overall retirement program.

We would not recommend "grandfathering" selected groups or picking any particular threshold point or cliff—it could work against you. Try to avoid locking into a conversion interest rate to any specific market rate. Try to look over a five- to ten-year period of what interest rates are averaging. By taking a longer-range view, you will have better success in that area.

Medical Plans Since the 1970s

Joseph J. Martingale
Vice President
Towers, Perrin, Forster & Crosby

American companies have been concerned about health care costs since the 1970s. As this concern has grown, corporate America has tried various approaches to managing health benefit costs by making changes in medical programs. We can actually identify three "eras" of change.

Risk-Shifting

Until the late 1970s, attention focused on financing and administrative arrangements; the movement away from insurance toward self-insurance had begun. This move toward self-insurance was driven by concerns about risk charges, premium taxes, and use of cash; and the preemption of state law by the Employee Retirement Security Act of 1974 (ERISA), which eased the burden of compliance with state regulations.

This era did see demonstrable savings on administration and premium taxes, and employers derived some real advantages from less need to comply with local regulations. A national employer could, for example, provide one benefits program at all locations.

The price for these advantages was a transfer of risk from the insurance company to the employer, particularly large and medium firms. Since the insurance company no longer bore the risk for rising health care costs, its incentive to contain its administrative costs disappeared. The risk shifted to the self-insured employer.

The Comprehensive Plan

In the early 1980s, health insurance research done by the Rand Corporation encouraged employers to redesign their benefit plans. They began to rethink levels of benefits, deductibles and co-insurance. In particular, they reconsidered paying more generous benefits for services delivered in a hospital than for services

received elsewhere. The base major medical plan—an extension of hospital insurance that only later evolved into an all-encompassing protection against health problems of all kinds—was redesigned to fit the times. We flattened the level of benefits and called it a comprehensive plan.

The comprehensive plan did eliminate that perverse incentive to treat patients in a more expensive setting. At the same time, plan redesign shifted some costs for health care to plan participants. Employers soothed their consciences by reasoning that this was not just a transfer of costs, it was educational. Plan participants would be more informed and prudent consumers of health care once they had the proper financial incentives.

The next step was utilization review. Although such review had been around for decades and was even adopted by Medicare, it began to gain prominence in the plans of a handful of large, self-insured employers. Employees had to precertify hospital admissions, and employers went wild requiring second surgical opinions. Many companies that implemented comprehensive plans adopted utilization review at the same time, asking employees to pay more of the costs and stressing the importance of becoming wiser health care consumers.

These plan design initiatives eased some of the employer's burden. And the introduction of utilization review was a critical first step toward more involvement in the delivery system by those who pay for the health care received. But the behavior of consumers did not change as much as hoped, and costs continued to soar. Senior management doubted the effectiveness of cost-saving efforts and demanded new initiatives.

Managed Care

These demands spurred the third era of change which began in the mid-1980s. Employers reluctantly acknowledged that they had to go beyond the familiar terrain of plan design, financing and administration into health care delivery. Often in desperation, employers added managed care networks to their plans.

During the first two eras, health maintenance organizations (HMOs) had grown dramatically, but benefits managers and others remained very skeptical of HMOs because of the complex way they were funded. The so-called "equal contribution" rule often forced employers to make overstated contributions to HMOs because they were not accounting for the younger, healthier employees who were enrolling in the HMOs.

So managed care arrived—as a last resort to many, with great trepidation for all, and with many mistakes along the way. Looking back, the move to managed care has been positive, but at the time, many feared the cost-effectiveness and quality of care of these network-based programs, as well as employee reactions to them. Nevertheless, several major national employers took the plunge, and the current era dawned.

What does the future hold for managed care programs and benefits plans that operate in a managed care environment? There is reason to think that managed care program costs will grow more slowly than traditional indemnity plans. Today, indemnity plan costs are rising at about 18 percent a year while managed care costs are more like 12 percent. But will this 6 percent difference be enough to satisfy CFOs and CEOs?

The networks are still developing; most have existed for only a few years, so there is enormous potential for improvement in the quality of care and in the efficiency of the system. With these improvements will come higher employee satisfaction and further cost reductions. But unless we can realize that potential, we will have to find something beyond managed care.

While we wait to see how managed care evolves, employers will continue to be involved in the health care delivery system. They will get more deeply involved in measuring the effectiveness and efficiency of the system, encouraging improvements in current networks, and incorporating smaller networks into employer-sponsored plans. Finally, they must create ways of ensuring profitability for those who operate efficiently and deliver quality health care to their employees.

Establishing a Managed Care Program

Kathleen O. Angel
Life and Health Benefits Manager
Digital Equipment Corporation

For the last 10 or more years, benefits managers have been using the skills they learned either within personnel departments or insurance companies to negotiate retention and risk and to manage the cost and efficiency of claims administration. The challenge of the 1990s will be for benefits managers to learn a different set of skills to develop close, personal relationships with individuals in the health care delivery system. Unless benefits managers work closely with the delivery system and control the health care dollars spent on that issue, employees will not get the most efficient plans.

About 50 percent of Digital Equipment Corporation's population is concentrated in the Northcast, especially Massachusetts and southern New Hampshire. We also have a few large pockets of employees in California, Colorado, and other states. In many of our sales offices, there are only 20 to 30 employees. This gives us a range of opportunities.

Investigating the Options

Prior to 1989, we had a typical 100 percent comprehensive medical plan. In 1990, we introduced a second indemnity plan along with some pre-tax options. This allowed the company to reconfigure our cost-sharing with employees, which had become disproportional over time, and gave employees some choice. But it did not help us with any long-term management of cost.

We started to look seriously into health care costs in 1987 when a committee of senior managers from various departments was formed to help formulate a long-term health care strategy. (That committee is still in existence.) First and foremost, we wanted to recognize our diverse work force and focus on employee choice. Second, although we had agreed on a managed care strategy, we wanted to be sure that we knew what it would mean for Digital.

We spent 1989 reading and studying, and talking to our employees and people at insurance companies and HMOs. Our policy towards HMOs until then had been very "hands off"; it was not part of the Digital plan. We did some financial checks and conducted some tests to make sure HMOs had adequate services, but we did not do any active management. We were able to get some utilization data thanks to the Washington Business Group on Health/Group Health Association of America Data Set from which we did some extrapolations. Those extrapolations, coupled with employee surveys that showed high satisfaction with HMOs (except for mental health and substance abuse), led us to start looking more favorably on them as a potential option.

P.O.S. Gains Digital Favor

Given the results of our research, we decided to focus our managed care strategy on HMOs, despite some real problems. First, only 30 percent of all our employees were enrolled in HMOs; for many others, HMOs were not going to be a palatable choice. Second, we saw opportunities for a point-of-service (P.O.S.) plan, but few HMOs were offering this. Our only choice was to negotiate with the highest quality HMOs we could locate in a given geographic region and to build our own P.O.S. network.

In 1990, my staff and I talked with four HMOs, three of which had never offered P.O.S. For the whole year we worked with those three group- and staff-model HMOs to actually design a P.O.S. program for Digital employees. We were fortunate because we have so many employees, making us an attractive target for HMOs. (We were also fortunate that HMO enrollment had slackened, so P.O.S. was an opportunity for growth for the HMOs.) However, there was a real concern from both network physicians and HMO management that P.O.S. would severely curtail their ability to manage people's health care. We had to convince them that Digital's objective was the same as theirs: to encourage our employees to stay within the system. If the HMOs and physicians were doing a good job, people would not want to opt out.

We are trying not to treat our P.O.S. plan, which we call HMO Elect, as a separate product within the HMOs. We figure the more streamlined it is, the fewer the chances of administrative snafus. Employees who opt for HMO Elect receive the same benefits as they would within an HMO, but they have the choice to receive care out-of-network. The plan design for out-of-network care is the same nationwide: As of 1992, there is a $300 deductible and a $3,000 out-of-pocket price tag.

We kept our two Digital indemnity plans and over 80 HMO offerings. For example, the Harvard Community Health Plan is offered as our HMO Elect partner for the eastern part of Massachusetts, but it is also offered as a lock-in HMO. In addition, we decided to keep all our preventive care programs including those in the indemnity and out-of-network programs. We felt that regardless of where people chose to take advantage of preventive care, we would support them, although ideally it would be within the HMO system.

In 1990, we also put out a request for pricing for what we called network management services. The network manager would help us build and develop our HMO network and help us in a hands-on way to manage the HMO partners we had selected for the P.O.S. program. We also needed them to pay out-of-network claims consistently. John Hancock Mutual Life Insurance Company was awarded the business; aside from knowing Digital through a previous relationship, this company showed flexibility in designing and staffing a group to handle the issues the way we wanted.

Continuing to Build

In 1991, our development year, we had 50 percent of our employees eligible for the four HMOs. By January 1992, we added 14 more sites in the United States, and 75 percent of our employees are now eligible. A full 73 percent of these employees opted for managed care. Because we built in rather strong incentives from a cost-sharing standpoint, we were anxious to implement similar systems everywhere as quickly as possible to avoid treating our employees differently in different locations.

Cost sharing has been one of the most challenging messages to communicate to employees. In reconfiguring our costs, we decided to base our cost sharing on the managed care model, essentially on the HMO. Previously, we had based the cost sharing of the indemnity plan on competitive data, deciding what percent the company would bear and what percent employees

would bear. Now employees opting to buy an indemnity plan will get the same dollars in subsidy from the company as they would if they had joined an HMO plan. HMO Elect is also slightly more expensive than an HMO plan because employees who choose the P.O.S. have the right to go to any system, but they have the obligation to pay for that choice.

In our 100 percent benefit plan (the indemnity plan), rates have jumped from $17.50 per week in 1990 to $59.00 in January 1992. Where we do not have HMO Elect, these rates are lower because we do not feel we can put in the cost-sharing strategy without providing a P.O.S. option. The company did not strive for cost savings the first year; it was an economic wash because the HMO rates were substantially reduced, reflecting the company's commitment to managed care.

Working With Networks

We have developed a set of quality standards, based on the principles of total quality management, which have been used to gauge over 20 HMOs for the past two years. By setting performance goals, we know whether they are improving, and we are beginning to assess the value of the money we spend.

The quality standards measure both technical quality of care and perception of care by employees. We ask the HMOs a number of questions including:

- What are their processes and structures to insure quality?

- Are they creating integrated, computerized records?

- Are they developing protocols internally for treatment?

- Do they monitor provider practices and the variations therein?

These questions help us understand how treatment and practice are linked.

At first, the physicians resisted these talks. But when they understood that we were trying to manage them according to the same principles that they were embracing and implementing in their own corporations, we developed a feeling of partnership. They have thanked us for being clear about what we expect of them.

Mental health and substance abuse received the lowest score from our employees in satisfaction about HMOs. We opted against carving out mental health because we wanted the HMOs to come up with a plan to better manage mental health benefits. We have articulated expectations that we want people to go through triage, to be individually assessed and case managed. Our idea is that we want all employees and their families to get the quality care they should in one setting.

Managed Care and
Widely Dispersed Employees

Charlene Rothkopf
Director of Benefit Operations
Marriott Corporation

Marriott operates in 4,200 locations across all 50 U.S. states. About 135,000 of our 200,000 employees are full-time and benefits-eligible; many of these are low-skilled, low-income and non-English speaking. Of that number, about 84,000 actually participate in a Marriott-sponsored benefit plan.

We had traditionally offered an indemnity program with four options which vary in deductibles, copayment levels, and out-of-pocket limits. We also had offered, in locations where available, a number of HMOs which proved very popular with employees.

As with most companies, we were experiencing a tremendous rise in our indemnity costs. In the three years prior to the full introduction of our managed care program, we had yearly increases of 20 to 25 percent in our indemnity plan, and the trend was continuing at least at that pace. We had already instituted pre-admission certification as well as second surgical opinion programs, and we felt deductibles were already as high as our employees could bear. From employee focus groups, we knew that choice, flexibility and quality were prime concerns, so we wanted to get all these with our managed care plan.

Our mission was, as of January 1990, to roll out a P.O.S. plan in as many locations as we could. We went through an extensive analysis to find the most appropriate locations. In January 1990, we rolled out 25 network locations. Five more were added in 1992.

We decided to go with one provider—the Prudential Insurance Company—to deliver our managed care program. The reason for this was that we wanted to have ease of administration and communication; we have a lot of people who transfer, so we felt with one carrier we would be able to minimize some of the problems. Even more important, because we are so spread out across the country and have no large presence in any one geographic area, we thought that one carrier could give us more leverage and negotiating power.

We offered Prudential's standard 90/70 P.O.S. plan, with a $10 office visit copayment. (That means 90 percent coverage for hospitalization within the network, 70 percent coverage out-of-network.) We also maintained our HMOs. So far, the P.O.S. plan has only replaced the indemnity plan in 30 locations; where we did not have networks or where the networks didn't meet our criteria, we have kept our indemnity plan.

Results to Date

We are currently undergoing a comprehensive evaluation through Johnson & Johnson Health Management, Inc. Our trend is still going up, but we think costs are below what they would have been without the managed care plan. Utilization of the P.O.S. plan was low for the first year because people were not sure exactly how it worked; we certainly saw a lot greater utilization in the second year of the program when we raised the employee contribution to the P.O.S. plan by 7.8 percent and the indemnity by 18 percent. In the P.O.S. plan, we found that, on average, 70 percent of our claims dollars are going in-network.

We also found that a lot of people have moved to the lock-in HMO after two years in the P.O.S. Before we introduced this plan, about 43 percent of employees participated in HMOs; this past year, the figure was up to 67 percent.

We do a random employee postcard survey to find out how the P.O.S. plan is working and if employees are satisfied. In general, we find that the HMOs get the highest satisfaction ratings. Why? Because they are easy to understand, and there are no claims forms to fill out. Because of the nature of our employee population, it is simply easier for our employees to access HMO care. The rating for the P.O.S. plans has gone up as people have gotten used to it. We continue to get the lowest rating in our indemnity plan because of the out-of-pocket expenses that people experience.

Lessons Learned

What have we learned through this two-year process? First, make sure that top management is knowledgeable about the program so they can support you if there is any negative employee reaction. We went to Marriott's top management and showed them where our indemnity was going, explained various alternatives, and outlined a number of the pros and cons of rolling out a managed care plan. We asked for their input and their concerns, and we identified the financial targets we hoped to reach and were accountable for.

Outside of the corporate executive staff, we wanted to make sure that we got as much local operation management support as we could. We really had to get out of our corporate offices and talk to the individual networks to make sure that we fully understood the local health care markets and how the networks operated. I think this is one key to a successful managed care program because each network does things a little bit differently; when problems occurred, our people needed to know who to contact. We also wanted to make sure they understood all the plan changes that were coming.

To lower resistance to change, we solicited employees' input about certain geographic areas. In some cases, we carved zip codes out of the network if our employees felt that there was limited coverage of providers in those areas. We identified areas where socioeconomic barriers might prevent some employees from going to a physician and areas where employees normally utilized services. For example, in the Washington, D.C. area, some people who live in Maryland will not travel into D.C. or Virginia to see a provider, even though travel time is only 10 or 15 minutes.

We also were able to identify regional differences in network operations, such as how many times you could change your physician or whether you can choose an obstetrician-gynecologist as a second primary care physician. We thought network operations were universal, but they really do differ by region. We made sure that those differences were fully explained to Marriott associates.

To address the quality issue, we did a qualitative audit of three networks. We had an outside consultant help us with this to make sure that the quality assurance and review aspects touted by the plan were really in place. In addition, we checked provider files to make sure they were being reviewed and updated on a regular basis.

Communications

Although people rationally understood why we were going to a P.O.S. plan, their emotional response was, "Is my doctor in the network or not?" There were many long-standing physician relationships and strong physician loyalty. There was a universal lack of understanding about how the health care system works, not to mention how managed care works. For example, people complained about the number of foreign doctors in the network. We had to show them that the percentage of foreign physicians was no different than in the medical community at large.

We found that the more education and understanding our people have, the higher the satisfaction rate with the plan. We used newsletters, posters, videos, handbooks and flash bulletins when something new was happening. We had specific communications about particular network areas. And again, most important were the face-to-face meetings held at the local networks. In fact, we held over 100 meetings in the first year to train people and inform them about changes. We also handled individual problems personally, responding to each distress signal.

Over the last couple of years, we have tried to create a "meeting of the minds" between Marriott and Prudential, our managed health care program administrators. We have worked very hard to develop a partnership with them—both a commitment to servicing our employees and to the care that is being provided. We have held team-building sessions, written a joint mission statement, and generally broken down some barriers to create more trust and honesty. In step with the need for joint responsibility for the success of the program, Prudential has openly discussed issues related to their operating expenses so that we can jointly determine how best to spend our administrative dollars.

Admittedly, we wanted big financial returns the first year, but there were some problems with moving that fast. With such short lead time, you don't have time to really get to know all of the networks and undergo the "due diligence" process that it takes to roll out a managed care plan well. For anyone attempting to try this, I would recommend they pilot the program first in a few networks to see how it goes and stagger the roll-out of any networks beyond that. I would also recommend on-site visits, staged over a period of time, to introduce the concept, to get feedback, and to come back with more information so that people have time to gradually accept the changes. Finally, and very important, take the time to network with other employers; we have found this to be invaluable.

Analyzing Medical Plan Performance

Jack E. Bruner

National Health Care Practice Leader
Hewitt Associates

The performance of health plans can be measured in three ways: by *perception*—what employees think is going on; by *process*—how well are the processes working and what is developing; and through *outcomes*—what the data claim actually happened.

In 1991, the perception process and performance audits we did doubled, and the number of outcome measurements jumped from 11 projects in 1990 to 187 projects in 1991. This proliferation of interest shows that companies are no longer managing health plans by anecdote but instead by fact-based decision-making.

What Makes Measurements Worthwhile?

What are some of the keys to success in data analysis? First, performance measurement cannot be a one-time event. Instead, it is a process that begins by measuring the issues most important to your customers, to the management that funds the plan, and to the employees that use health care plans. Second, to be successful, measurement must focus on viable opportunities for improvement; it does little good to measure things which cannot be addressed.

The use of benchmarking to provide direction and focus is a third key to success in data analysis. Comparing yourself to norms in an environment where most employers are dissatisfied with the results is hardly practical. We found the most aggressive approaches used in the various areas of health management differ substantially from the norms. A fourth key to success is communicating with both the care providers and employees. Managing the carrier relationships and improving employee satisfaction with those relationships clearly defines needs, giving direction to your service providers so they can attain superior results. The measurement of performance leads you to begin the cycle again. This measurement is not meant to decide whether or not the plan was successful, but to support a continuous improvement process by determining which parts of the plan are working and which are not.

The technical evolution of measuring health plan performance has moved forward at a fairly dramatic pace in the last several years. The data, however, are only half the story; the other half is having the expertise to interpret the data. Among the organizations we have worked with, the most successful in attacking health issues are those that involve not only design experts, but experts in finance, clinical issues, and even the claim-paying groups to provide a variety of viewpoints in interpreting data.

Data on Regions and Group Demographics

Sometimes it is not a matter of the underlying data telling you something but rather how the data are coded. You can have the largest comparative database in the world, but it will not be fully effective unless the information can be broken down and disseminated for comparison purposes. If you have your comparative database adjusted correctly, you can see quickly where your plan is performing well and where there are aberrations on which to focus.

One of the most dramatic evolutions in the analysis of data and plan performance is the concept of measuring episodes of care as opposed to individual claims. Individual claims are like pieces in a puzzle: They do not tell you much by themselves. For instance, you cannot tell how efficient a primary care physician is unless you know what services he or she has provided, the outcome of the care, the hospital services and tests that were utilized along the way, and the specialists that became involved in the process.

Total costs per claim, total costs per incidence as well as rates of change are also pertinent. These tell you which initiatives implemented in a given year worked to reduce costs and which did not. They may also clarify where the emerging threats may be.

The ability to categorize by location, option, provider and employee group is critical. Many employers look at managed care as a uniform solution to be implemented across populations. But as they begin to separate the data, they see that particular problems are focused in particular geographic locations. Without disrupting the employees in other locations, they can get 80 percent of the benefit, for instance, of the managed mental health plan by focusing on two problem locations. We believe that, through health-risk appraisal data and additional claim data, in five years we will be talking about case managing before the medical disaster occurs.

Maintaining an Employee Focus

Management's definition of success has changed fairly radically. A few years ago, we would present a menu of alternatives, choices would be made, and we would move forward. The challenge is balancing the concern for the bottom line while keeping employees happy and quality high.

As insurance companies and carriers have moved away from claims administration and into the delivery of care through managed care, we have observed that there have been significant disruptions in their operations. The results of our audits have declined significantly, particularly in the managed care area; for the first firms that went into these arrangements, there are at least three programming or documentation errors in every instance where we have audited the program. It is at the point where our clients are doing pre-audits; they actually audit the carrier programming, staffing and documentation before the programs are launched so that they do not have unhappy employees. In administration we are demanding much more of the insurance carriers and the organizations that manage networks. Focusing on ways of having zero defect or very effective implementation methodologies in administration are critical to the future.

From an employee-needs perspective, listening exercises have yielded some startling results. We recently ran a focus group in which we presented three alternatives to employees: additional cost sharing, managed care concepts, or managing health. Some employees are not excited about any of these alternatives. But the bottom line was that, as we move beyond deductibles and some of the financial measures, we are getting into people's lives. Employees want to be sure that solid facts back up any managed health or managed care initiative and that quality is not a secondary consideration. We cannot fool anyone; our employees know that cost is driving management's agenda, so we have to reinforce that quality is an important part of the equation. Data is one of the most credible ways of accomplishing that.

To satisfy both management and employees, we must find ways to control costs instead of just shifting them. If we look at every decision made in the health care process to try to come up with a zero defect approach, savings could be achieved without cost shifting. The opportunities available from illness prevention and early intervention are nearly equivalent to those provided by managed care but require a much tougher discipline and return on investment approach to managing health than we have had in the past.

While it is not practical to believe that you can eliminate 45 percent of costs in one year, we see organizations across the board hitting 5 to 8 percent; they try to get 1 or 2 percent out of each of 5 or 6 areas each year and just keep after it in the process. They seem to be able to manage the change in a way that employees can live with.

The keys to data analysis or measuring plan performance are to first establish a baseline or current position. Second, focus on customer needs—both management and employees—and try to create win/win situations. Third, look at areas that you can change as opposed to those you cannot influence. Finally, target best practice strategies. Do not look at the norms but at the top performers across industries to see where implemented changes will have the greatest impact.

Measuring Medical Plan Administration Performance

Kenneth J. Morrissey
Manager, Corporate Employee Benefits
FMC Corporation

Today, the quest for quality is paramount. Most of the time when we think of quality we think in terms of tangible goods. But quality principles can also be applied to the health insurance administration area. Quality in health care administration is performance as perceived by the customer, not necessarily the standards set by the administrator.

Quality is usually measured relative to the competition, but you also need to differentiate from the competition if you are going to be successful. For example, an on-line computer system ties together our claims administrator's customer service staff and our local plant human resource staff. This provides standardized answers to questions regularly posed to the customer service staff by our employees or their medical providers. This technology creates an element of consistency that contributes to accurate answers with a high degree of customer satisfaction.

We have imposed seven performance standards on our claims administrator as part of our contract. Six of these deal directly with the administration of claims:

1) *Payment dollar accuracy:* All claims processed must have an average annual accuracy of 99 percent or better. This is simply measured by dividing the dollar amount of claims paid accurately by the total dollars paid.

2) *Coding accuracy:* The appropriate medical procedure coding must be applied to at least 99 percent of all processed claims. In our experience with a previous claims administrator, about half of our data was rejected for analysis purposes because the coding was either in error or omitted.

3) *Claims turnaround time:* Eighty percent of all claims must be resolved within nine calendar days starting from the day the claim is received, including weekends and holidays.

4) *Subrogation referral:* A separate firm administers our subrogation efforts. We reward our administrator monetarily for claims identified as having recovery potential. This year we will be approaching $1 million in subrogation recovery. (In early 1991, the Supreme Court affirmed that the ERISA preempts state laws in subrogation issues [*FMC v. Holliday*].)

5) *Coordination of benefits:* Our standard is 13.5 percent of claims dollars recovered for medical and 6 percent for dental. Actual claim dollars recovered in 1990 was 15 percent for medical and 5 percent for dental. In real-dollar terms, this amounted to $10 million.

6) *Claim payment nonperformance:* In the event our claims administrator fails to process claims, we not only have the right to cancel the contract, but the administrator must also pay our transition costs to a new administrator.

Keeping Employees and Retirees Satisfied

Employee satisfaction is the seventh and final performance standard category. Based on a claims satisfaction survey distributed to claimants, responses should show that 98 percent of our employees and retirees are satisfied by the level of service. Since the claims administrator logs in all claims on our computer system, they know at all times what claims are coming in. We then select 1 out of every 20 claimants as survey participants.

The original objective of the survey was to measure employee satisfaction with the administrator's service, but there were some secondary objectives, too. First, specific claims processing problems are identified. If a survey has comments and if the respondent included his or her name and Social Security number, the administrator does a follow-up.

Also, due to employee reaction, we made a number of improvements to the administration processes. For example, we redesigned the claim form to reduce mistakes and lessened the claim form requirements to reduce the number of claim transactions. We also published several articles in employee newsletters in response to items that frequently recurred in the survey. A computerized benefit information system, mentioned earlier, enabled us to standardize the answers to typical employee benefit questions.

What has happened so far in the survey? For the first nine months of 1991, we had about 84,000 claimants; about 5 percent (approximately 4,000 people) were selected, almost half of whom returned the survey. (Retirees are returning the survey at a substantially higher rate than active employees.) If a survey respondent answers either "excellent" or "good" as opposed to "fair" or "poor" to the question, "Please rate your overall satisfaction with the administrator's service," we count that as a positive response. Over the first nine months, there was a substantial increase in the level of employee satisfaction.

Our survey also asks a number of specific questions about employees' perceived level of claims service. Besides the overall level of service, it asks questions such as, "Are claims paid promptly?" The survey shows that 80 percent of our people feel that claims are paid promptly. Our claims turnaround time in January 1991 was 13 days, and right now it is 8 days. That is a substantial improvement, yet employee perception has yet to catch up with this fact.

All the measurement standards we have implemented have enabled us to ensure that our employees (and retirees) receive a high level of claims administration service.

Measuring Medical Plan Performance

Ron Z. Goetzel

Director, Data Analysis and Evaluation Services
Johnson & Johnson Health Management, Inc.

Johnson & Johnson Health Management, Inc., has just concluded an evaluation of a large American firm whose per-employee medical costs had increased by 217 percent between 1979 and 1985. In response, this company developed a P.O.S. managed care program which was first offered in the second quarter of 1987. Employees within network cities have a choice of either enrolling in the HMOs available within that city or in the P.O.S. plan.

When in the P.O.S. plan, employees have a choice of using a network or non-network provider. There are positives and negatives involved in either choice: If individuals choose a network provider, their care is essentially covered at 100 percent with no claim forms; there is a $10 copayment for outpatient care. If they choose a non-network provider, there is a deductible, co-insurances and out-of-pocket expense.

The company chose a new firm to administer the P.O.S. plan, and Johnson & Johnson was selected to evaluate the program. We conducted a study looking at a five-year period: 2.5 years under the old plan and 2.5 years under the new one. Data came from a variety of sources including both the new and old administrators, a mail-order drug firm, the company's enrollment files, HMO enrollment, cost data accumulated and aggregated from 52 different HMOs around the country, and normative data from the National Center for Health Statistics. This study was conducted as a true cost-benefit analysis because not only did it consider how much the company paid out, but it also considered the administrative costs incurred from both administrators. We were not just looking at the overall paid amounts: We were looking at the cost of administering, managing and running the program.

The evaluation centered on the company's largest subsidiary, which has about 95 percent of the employees and an equal percent of paid benefit dollars. We looked at when people actually received the care as opposed to when the claims were paid. Consequently, there was a longer lag period between when a claim is actually processed and when it got in the system and could be evaluated. We also created two distinct databases. The first was an aggregate database that included all expenses incurred from indemnity, HMO and administrative fees. The second was based on the experience of a cohort population: The same people were tracked over the entire five years, creating a unique microcosm of the company's population. Roughly 85 percent of the people remained in that cohort over the five years.

How do you go about assessing the results of a program? The only way you can truly assess it is by looking at what actually happened versus what is expected. The difference between the two equals the savings.

A Basis for Comparison

We did not conduct a traditional tracking study—taking snapshots over time and then assessing them. (This is an inaccurate assessment system, and it makes it difficult to draw conclusions because there are many factors which go unaccounted.) Instead, we applied a statistical technique called multiple regression analysis which essentially subtracts out "confounders," other factors in the environment that may affect change.

What are some of these factors? One is demographic shifts; populations change over time, and as employees grow older or as more women enter the population, your costs are affected. For example, as men age, they become more expensive than women. Women, on the other hand, are expensive in their childbearing years, but their costs do not increase as steeply as men's as they grow older.

A second factor is HMO migration. When the P.O.S. plan was communicated to the employees, many turned to the HMO instead. This affected costs. Third is the growing number of retirees. A fourth factor is change in the type of coverage; if single individuals move to family coverage, this, too, will affect costs.

The multiple regression model subtracts out all these other factors and tells you the independent effects of the managed care program. Do these factors really make a difference? Let's take HMO migration as an example. In the first year that the company introduced its P.O.S. plan, HMO enrollment increased by 150 percent. The migrants were generally younger, female, non-management and single. Consequently, the regression analyses calculated that for every 10 percent migration to HMO, the company realized a 3.7 percent increase in its overall costs. Had the increase not been subtracted from the equation, it would have been attributed to the managed care program. It also turned out that migrants averaged out to be roughly $300 cheaper than the people remaining in the indemnity plan.

When we compared actual with expected costs after removing all the confounders, we found that, on average, the P.O.S. plan resulted in costs that were 13 percent lower than expected. The company saw roughly a 25 percent savings from a dramatic reduction in in-patient utilization. These were offset somewhat by an 8 percent increase in outpatient care. Overall, increases before network implementation were running at about 12 percent; after implementation they were about 6 percent on an annual basis.

Johnson & Johnson's studies are different because the outcome variable is total cost, not just the indemnity costs. We use multiple regression methodology, different types of comparisons, and a cohort database. These techniques aid in formulating accurate and complete conclusions related to managed care program effects.

Retiree Health Plans

Peter J. Dowd
Regional Practice Leader, Health & Welfare Consulting
Ernst & Young

I have seen an enormous change since the late 1970s in retiree health plans. At that time, companies gave these benefits away, making plans richer and richer. That continued until 1984 when court cases and rumors about the Financial Accounting Statement (FAS) 106 exposure draft began the age of cutbacks. We must realize that FAS 106 focused on the problem but did not cause it. Many of us resent that our generation must deal with removing the transition obligation that has been building up.

While we are struggling with this reshaping, we cannot overlook the needs of retirees. For retirees, advancing age means advancing medical costs, and many active employees expect to carry their benefits into retirement, which is not necessarily the case anymore.

As we cut back, we must realize that retirees cannot handle cost shifting as effectively as active employees because benefits make up a much greater percentage of their household income. If you think of potentially canceling or discontinuing this coverage, you will find that retirees are probably willing to pay stiff contributions for the security of knowing that they won't have to pick up catastrophic losses.

In addition, many plans are starting to reconsider their philosophies toward spouse coverage. If you look at the overall liability of any specific retiree, adding the spouse to that liability will probably increase costs by 120 to 170 percent because that spouse might be younger and could potentially live longer.

From a funding standpoint, the majority of employers are still waiting for a miracle "cure." Employers are considering buying the liability back from retirees at less than market share, VEBA, 501(c)9 trusts, 401(h), 401(k), employee stock ownership plans, and either corporate-owned or trust-owned life insurance. We may have seen the last of corporate-owned life insurance if the tax deductibility of the loans against cash value is taken away.

Why Offer Long Term Care Insurance?

Robert W. Sears
Director-Actuarial, Benefits and Compensation
Coopers & Lybrand

The United States has an expanding population of about 31.8 million people over age 65.

The 80-and-older group is the fastest growing segment of the U.S. population. About 60 percent of those over age 65 are female, but 85 percent of those over age 85 are female. This population will become increasingly important in terms of purchasing power and the need for long term care.

Let's look at the issue from another perspective: About 4.5 percent of people 65-and-over are in a nursing home, and another 12.2 percent are disabled and living in the community. All total, about 1.7 million people use nursing homes, and 4.4 million are disabled but remain in the community.

Most long term care costs fall to those over age 80. In their lifetime, about 15 percent of people over 65 will incur costs greater than $80,000 for long term care; 15 percent of nursing home entrants begin as private-paid patients but become Medicaid eligible, and 35 percent of nursing home entrants receive Medicaid within their first month of residence.

A study conducted by the Washington Business Group on Health in October 1991 asked 200 of the Fortune 500 corporations in the United States what they intend to do with long term care benefits in their corporations. About 26 percent of respondents said that they plan on offering long term care within two years; over 75 percent plan on offering long term care sometime in the next five years. Approximately 10 percent of the responding companies currently sponsor group long term care plans.

There are a variety of reasons why some corporations are uncertain about what they are going to do. One reason is unfavorable tax treatment; another is that some corporations do not see much concern among their employees about long term care. Although fewer firms may actually address long term care than the survey indicates, the long term care market has exploded. In 1987, two corporations had long term care offerings; in 1991 there were well over 100. The reason many corporations are offering long term care is that they expect their employees to plan ahead for their retirement, and this is one way for them to do that.

Very few corporations offering long term care contribute toward the cost of the package; in most corporations it is an employee-pay-all product. A number of corporations offering long term care are significant in their size, including General Electric Company, IBM Corporation, AEtna Life & Casualty Company, State of Alaska, Bell Atlantic Corporation, American Express Company, General Motors Corporation, Monsanto Company, BellSouth Corporation, Chevron Corporation, and The Procter & Gamble Company. Although long term care tends to be offered by large employers, this may change in the near future as more medium-size employers begin to offer it as well.

Creating and Communicating Long Term Care Programs

Barry R. Busch
Consultant, Insurance Plans
General Electric Company

General Electric Company's long term care insurance program became effective on May 1, 1992, for active employees, their spouses, parents and parents-in-law. As soon as the enrollment for active employees is completed, the plan will be rolled out to retirees, and their plan will become effective on July 1.

GE has about 220,000 active employees, 35 percent of whom are unionized, plus about 135,000 retirees distributed across all 50 states. Even though we are highly diversified and decentralized, almost all our people are covered under the same benefit program which includes life insurance, health benefits, pension and savings, most of which are employer-funded. We also offer a wide array of optional plans such as life insurance, long-term disability, personal accident, and flexible spending account. This market-basket approach has worked well since it allows our employees to select the combination of benefits that best meets individual and family needs.

It was the logical step to add long term care to our market basket. When we first looked at the issue in 1987, we concluded that it was still too new, posing too many unanswerable questions. In the summer of 1990, we revisited the product. At that time, long term care was getting a lot of attention in the media. In addition, we got a strong sense from our employees, retirees and unions that a long term care benefit would meet a real need and that GE sponsorship would be viewed very favorably. With senior management's agreement to proceed, we moved to phase two: to select a carrier and decide on a plan design.

Designing a Plan

We began by inviting four insurance companies to recommend a plan design for GE. During interviews with the companies, we pressed hard for their latest thinking in the field. We considered a variety of options, including reasonable-and-customary versus schedule benefits. We looked at whether schedules of benefits based on services rendered made sense versus the traditional daily benefit option. We looked at indemnity models versus disability models.

After we felt that we understood the consequences of the varying approaches, we put together our own plan design which drew from the best thinking of each of the carriers. While many of the provisions of our plan are consistent with those of IBM Corporation and AT&T Company, there are some differences that we adopted because we thought they were particularly important (see box on page 32).

Although our benefit changes following union negotiations typically take effect on January 1, we determined that in order to maximize the enrollment in long term care it needed to be offered separately. We also wanted sufficient lead time to do it right. We selected May 1, 1992, for active employees and July 1 for retirees.

Choosing the Right Carrier

After we had developed our plan design and time frame, we submitted a request for proposal (RFP) to each of the four insurance carriers who had recommended plan designs. Our evaluation criteria focused on seven key points:

- the carrier's vision and capability to manage changes in the marketplace over time;

- their top management's commitment to the line of business;

- low rates with long-run stability;

Key Elements of General Electric's Long Term Care Plan

- Our eligible group includes employees, their spouses, parents and spouses' parents. Retirees and spouses, and surviving spouses of both employees and retirees will also be offered the coverage. We have no minimum or maximum age under the plan. Employees will be given insurance on a guaranteed issue basis; all other applicants will be underwritten.

- All persons eligible for insurance will be given a choice of a nursing-home-only option or a comprehensive option. The nursing home option is about half the cost of the comprehensive option. The comprehensive option covers 100 percent of room and board charges for nursing home stays up to the daily limit. It also reimburses 100 percent of the most common charges for home care: case management, skilled nursing and custodial care in the home, adult day care, and up to 21 days a year for respite care.

- The GE plan offers four nursing home daily benefit options: $50, $100, $150 and $200 per day. The home care benefit is 50 percent of the daily benefit amount.

The $200 per day benefit is unique, and we offered it for two reasons. First, we felt it was responsive to people who lived in high-cost areas. Second, it allows an individual to purchase a higher amount of coverage than they need today (at their current age), thus enabling them to defer upgrading their coverage at a higher cost at some time in the future.

- In order to qualify for benefits, an individual must meet three out of seven activities of daily living (ADLs) which include bathing, dressing, eating, transferring, mobility, toileting and continence. Our waiting period is 60 days of receiving covered services in a nursing home and 30 days for home care. Premium is waived once benefits begin.

- We offer two nonforfeiture benefits: a death benefit which is based on a refund of contributions and a reduced paid-up feature which vests benefits from 30 percent to 75 percent based on the number of years an individual contributed to the plan. If one contributed for 10 years and stopped, the benefit would be 30 percent. Three percent would be vested each year after 10.

- the depth of their personnel;

- their systems' capabilities;

- their willingness to devote resources to minimize the effort that GE would have to expend on the implementation; and

- the long-term financial stability of the carrier.

We found it relatively easy to evaluate the carriers based on these criteria, but we had difficulty understanding the differences in rates. We had to put together a separate RFP for the financial aspects of the plan in order to make sense of the disparity among the rates of the bidders. Although all the carriers were fairly close and of very high quality, we selected Metropolitan Life Insurance Company.

Setting the Plan in Motion

We had to negotiate the plan with our unions, which turned out to be relatively easy since, when we were at the bargaining table, the union made a presentation to us for this coverage. Following negotiations, we established two work teams, one to deal with communicating and implementing the plan both internally and externally, the other to deal with enrollment.

The communication team had two major assignments: 1) to develop the promotional and descriptive material for employees and retirees; and 2) to make sure that all HR personnel within our 13 businesses understood, supported and were prepared to do their part in communicating the plan. In the past, the corporate

office typically came up with the plan and gave it out to the businesses. This time everyone participated.

We put the Met Life senior account executive on a plane to personally visit each of the 13 businesses. At each location, she described the plan, answered questions, and sought the business unit input on the communications strategies. Met Life set up a separate phone number for the HR people so that they could immediately get answers to questions from Met Life. The input from HR turned out to be critical to all parties involved because it helped us to structure the 800-lines, the newsletter articles, videotapes and enrollment materials in such a way that it maximized everyone's effectiveness.

At the same time, a separate group of Met Life and GE representatives focused on enrollment and administrative issues. Employees and spouses can enroll over the phone using the same system we use for some of our other benefits. We have payroll deductions for employees, and spouses will have the option of either being payroll deducted or directly billed. Retirees' payments can be pension deducted or directly billed. All others will be directly billed.

Things have gone extremely well so far. In fact, we have had no problems at all. Allowing over a year for lead time probably helped. Besides the long lead time, the other aspect of our process that has worked well has been securing HR personnel buy-in. Because they are the ones "on the firing line" at the local level, they need to understand the plan and to feel that they are getting the full support of both our carrier and corporate staff.

IBM's Long Term Care Program

Edward J. Shugrue
Director, Employee Benefits
International Business Machines Corporation

In 1986 our HR staff conducted a sample survey of IBM employees to better understand attitudes toward work/life issues and to help the company understand our employees' needs. One section of the survey was devoted to balancing work and personal life. The data collected suggested that caring for others was a significant component of our employees' lives:

- Thirty percent of our employees had some responsibility for the care of others, not including children;

- about 8.9 percent had responsibility for adult dependents;

- 5.2 percent had adult dependents living elsewhere; and

- 3.7 percent had adult dependents living in their homes.

A follow-up study in 1991 indicated that the number of employees who may have a need for long term care would continue to grow.

These results started us thinking about the long term care problems our employees were facing. We concluded that they could benefit from a long term care program that might include services ranging from adult day care to home nursing care.

In addition to the questionnaire and demographics studies, we felt our employees were ready for a long term care program. Expanded media coverage was adding to employee understanding and heightening their concern about the long term care responsibilities that they and their families might face in the future. Through the media, they were becoming aware of the potential magnitude of the long term care expenses, and they began to realize that they would not be covered under traditional sources such as our own company-based programs and Medicare.

A third factor in our decision was the diversity of our work force, their families and retirees. Actually, this influenced our design, not whether or not we would do it. In 1986 we had a population of about 200,000 active employees in the United States and 40,000 retirees. So we knew that the concerns we needed to address would vary considerably. For example, a long term care program would primarily be used by our retirees, catastrophically ill employees, or active employees who suffer serious injury. This meant we required a flexible program with several different options. That became the beginning of our design phase.

Serving Employee and Corporate Needs

During the design phase we also realized that the plan had to be cost-effective for both our employees and the company. We knew that cost would be a major factor in employees' ability to participate, but the company wanted to incur minimal additional expense. Finally, we wanted our program to expand employee responsibility for their financial well-being (shared responsibility) both pre- and post-retirement. Shared responsibility has been a particularly important part of design changes in IBM's benefits plans since the late 1980s. Our role is to educate employees on the need to plan for the future and to present them with existing options.

We assembled a team from the employee benefits staff along with a consultant. They designed a plan which meets all our objectives. Features include:

- *Flexiblility.* The plan has three daily benefit options and different coverage services from home health care to respite care to adult day care and nursing home care.

- *Broad eligibility.* Regular full- and part-time employees, spouses, employee's parents if the employee participates, parents-in-law if the spouse participates, and retirees and their spouses are eligible.

- *Cost consideration.* An inflation adjustment factor may be offered every three years as needed.

- *Informed resources.* A case management feature insures that when our employees do access the program they get the best advice.

- *Affordability.* There is a premium reimbursement by IBM. While our offering is employee-pay-all, employees, retirees and their spouses are eligible for up to 20 percent reimbursement of their annual premium through the personal health provision of our major medical plan.

In addition, we have the ability to adapt the offering based on experience. For example, we could decrease the amount of time an employee must wait before receiving the benefit, or we could increase the number of daily benefit options beyond what we have now. We have also retained flexibility to adapt our program in case government legislation should affect it in the future.

Promoting the Plan

Communication was probably the most difficult aspect of the entire process because of the number of offerings for employees and the limited resources available to distribute to the various plans. We introduced our long term care insurance program in the summer of 1990 when we announced several other changes to our health benefit plans. We thought this would be the appropriate time to introduce both the program and the concept of long term care because we already had the entire U.S. work force focused on benefit projection and planning.

We used several communications tools to help our employees understand the subject. In addition to the description of the long term care plan contained in our health benefits announcement, John Hancock developed a comprehensive brochure, which was distributed by a home mailing to all eligible populations. The home mailing also contained a postcard that could be used to request a copy of a 10-minute videotape for home viewing. We felt it was important for the employees to have the program information at home where they could discuss it with family members, since long term care situations typically affect the entire family.

We also had location meetings so employees and retirees could hear more about long term care, ask questions about it, and view the video. These meetings were conducted at our sites across the United States by IBM benefits administrators and members of John Hancock. We found that the early enrollment results were much higher at locations where we had meetings where both *IBMers* and members of the John Hancock team were available to answer questions.

From the beginning, John Hancock established a toll-free number specifically for the IBM plan. We also ran two spots about our long term care program on our internal television network which broadcasts daily news to IBM locations across the country. We timed these television spots to coincide with the first anniversary of our long term care offering. When we tracked the response to the television shows, we found a sharp increase in inquiries and requests for information kits to the toll-free number at John Hancock following each broadcast.

We worked with John Hancock recently to design and distribute a brochure specifically targeting our retirees, answering their most frequently asked questions about long term care. We have seen an immediate four-fold increase in weekly requests for information kits.

We believe that our offering has been quite successful because it provides both flexibility and affordability. Our employees have choices for managing the uncertainty of long term care costs. We have tried to make it easy for them in the process. Finally, we think we can respond appropriately to the needs of our diverse population in a changing and dynamic world.

The Changing Role of the Benefits Manager

Donald F. Crowley
Division Head, Compensation and Benefits
Citibank, N.A.

Manufacturing provides a lesson in how to manage a field like benefits, which requires knowledge of many specialized and arcane subjects. Until recently, the product design cycle started with research and development; concepts created for products, materials and devices were passed along to advanced engineering. They in turn passed along the idea to design engineering, who created the product specifications. These then flowed into manufacturing, where the engineers created the processes to make the product. Once manufacturing started, distribution, field service and more engineers got involved in areas like rigging, packaging and service.

In many cases, the cost to fix a mistake if caught in the design phase was a unit of one (say, $1). If manufacturing discovered the problem, the cost multiplied by 10 ($10) for the same mistake. Finally, if field service discovered the error, it was $100, not to mention the negative customer effect. The message is, catch problems in the early stages of design.

Today, it is common for all the appropriate engineers to work at the front end of design; the design and manufacturing engineers are now working with distribution, quality control and field service. They are part of a team, typically led by a product or program manager. This method of cooperative work means no surprises and collective ownership of a product.

The same principle can be applied to benefits. In the past, the benefits designers would create programs needed by the company. After receiving approval from the management team, the program was sprung—basically without warning—on the company accountants, lawyers, employees and unions, among others. Too often problems were fixed "in the field." If other people

---

Questions Benefits Professionals Should Be Asking Themselves

- **Compensation:** Have we thought about total compensation? If our ratio of direct versus indirect costs is not where we want it, what is our strategy to get there?

- **Benefits design:** Are we listening to our own people? Have we paid attention to attitude surveys? Have we talked to or conducted a grievance analysis with the union? Do we know where the issues are coming from?

- **Existing programs:** Do we understand how our programs work and the implications this has for the future? What is our response to that? Are we willing to let the programs shape themselves, or are we actively designing future programs?

- **Assets/liabilities:** Have we adjusted our asset allocations strategy to reflect the asset/liability analysis that we have modeled?

- **Managing our managers:** Are we really on top of management performance or are we wedded to a handful of money managers who are not judged by their performance?

- **Financials:** Given FAS 106, are we striking the right balance between our obligations to today's and tomorrow's shareholders? Are we maximizing short-term performance at the expense of the long term?

- **Communications:** What is our strategy for allowing employees access to HR and benefits information?

- **Legislation:** Are we where we need to be with ERISA, labor, employment and SEC laws? Health care legislation is on its way in the 1990s; are we "in the know" about that?

- **Medical community:** Are we collaborating with doctors? Do we have doctors working with us on medical design or medical analysis? Is the collaboration a partnership?

Launching New Benefits Programs

PHASE	Requirements Planning	Design	Management Approval	Pre-Launch	Communication & Implementation
PARTIES/FUNCTIONS INVOLVED	• Business Planners • Total Compensation Strategies • Employee Listening Studies/Grievance Analysis • Dialogue Union Leaders • Dialogue HR Heads • Benefits Professionals	• Benefits Professionals • Lawyers • Accountants • Systems Experts • Actuaries • Medical Directors • Carriers	• Senior Managment	• Employee Focus Groups – Communications • Systems Debugging • Management Infrastructure	• Employees • Unions

had been involved earlier, the program launch would have been much simpler and the product far better.

Creating Partnerships for Increased Productivity

Planning for needs and prelaunching are two excellent ideas for newcomers. In requirements planning, we consider company strategies and tactics and decide on the role of each "part" of compensation—benefits, pay and other perquisites. We have listened to our employees, talked with HR and the unions, and have all the company requirements on the table before the first design pencil hits the paper. Benefits professionals are very much a part of this meeting, often driving the process.

Once the product is approved by management and we enter prelaunch, "debugging" begins. We conduct systems tests and polish employee communications through focus groups. After all this work, the launch becomes anticlimactic (see chart, above).

Looking at benefits design and management in the 1990s, one word describing the new model comes to mind: "partnership." We have to be more open and involve specialists because we cannot be on the cutting-edge in every issue area. We must have shared ownership of products and their launch.

What Benefits Managers Will Need to Know

Burkett W. Huey, Jr.
Director, Benefits
PepsiCo Incorporated

Michael A. Tarre
Director, Corporate Compensation and Benefits
International Business Machines Corporation

Major changes have occurred in the benefits profession recently. The role of the benefits manager used to be an administrator, a caretaker of plans. Today, benefit managing is enormously important to businesses and to employees. From 1970 to 1990, benefits as a percentage of wages rose from 11.5 percent to 19.9 percent. The impact of post-retirement welfare in many companies is going to be in the millions and, in some cases, in the billions of dollars. Benefits have replaced wages as a major strike issue. With mergers, reorganizations and bankruptcies, security and the preservation of benefits have acquired new meaning and importance for employees.

As a result, benefits managers have a broader, more strategic job requiring additional skills. A benefits manager needs to be well-schooled in law, tax and finance, accounting and medical practice; skills such as medical economics, statistical analysis, computer technology, communications and advertising are also crucial. (This is in addition to all the traditional skills of actuarial analysis, insurance practices, regulations and buttoned-down administration.) As business has moved overseas, benefits managers have had to acquire different kinds of skills as well, including more knowledge about business practices, regulations, value systems, cultures (and even languages) of countries other than the United States.

Changing to Meet New Challenges

So what does the benefits field require today? First, it seems there is no natural reason why college graduates would choose benefits as a career. Throughout the 1980s, benefits departments were blessed with an influx of very talented women because HR was an open door for them into business. That door is no longer the only one. As a result, benefits departments will have to compete for talent, recruiting like any other department or profession.

Second, benefits managers must raise their professional standards and hire and promote against them. The technical skills need to be applied to strategic goals and focuses, as well as tactical ones. Goals must be defined in business terms. Benefits will gain respect from other business professions by adding value to the solutions of business problems, not by pretending that they have nothing to do with business.

Third is communications. Benefits are complex, but the programs are meaningless unless they are communicated in simple and clear terms. This is true for employees who will ignore or discount anything that is not clearly communicated and equally true for senior management who will pay no heed to concepts with a less-than-clear focus.

The future of benefits management is in our hands. If we attract and grow talented people, we will prosper and thrive. If we do not, at best our function will return to being benefits administration; at worst, it will disappear.
— *Burkett W. Huey, Jr.*

IBM recently completed a study on the worldwide human resources function to identify priorities for creating competitive advantage for our corporation. To do this, we surveyed 3,000 individuals around the world—HR and line executives, and university faculty members.

Respondents from both line management and HR agree that HR will be more critical to company success by the year 2000. Also, the role of the HR professional will become increasingly strategic instead of operational—more proactive instead of reactive—in developing programs and solutions.

We also looked at the role line management will play in benefits in the future. Whether good news or bad, the line manager will emerge as a partner, with benefits managers becoming more like business partners with an advice and counsel role to line management. Within each area of importance to the benefits community—strategy, program development, program management and communications—we expect that the line will be more involved and share more responsibility with personnel and the HR function by the year 2000.

A number of challenges were uncovered as well. Responses show that benefits managers are going to have to do a better job influencing line management by demonstrating the financial impact of decisions. They will need to be more computer literate and more effective at anticipating changes. In addition, they will need a broader knowledge of HR functions.

From an organizational viewpoint, benefits management will be organized around work to be done; issues and specific projects will supersede a particular functional orientation. The profile of benefits professionals in flexible organizations will include people who have rotational types of assignments and experience in other key business areas; are generalists rather than specialists; are multilingual, globally oriented, and have financial expertise with a focus on the future.

My vision of future benefits managers is that they will be pivotal in shaping tomorrow's work force and will channel value to employees at optimal cost to the company. If we take on these challenges, I believe we will continue to have a major influence on our companies, giving them a competitive advantage in the 21st century.

— Michael A. Tarre

The Changing Role for Insurers

John D. Moynahan, Jr.

Executive Vice President

Metropolitan Life Insurance Company

The United States is at a significant crossroad. Some of the challenges we face are internal while others are external; some challenges are near term, such as the recession, while others are long term and will likely prove more intractable, such as the enormous budget deficit and international competition in both the manufacturing and service sectors.

Regardless of where the challenges lie, improved productivity from workers is at the heart of the solution. In speaking of improved worker productivity, we must talk of improving the incentives to increase productivity—our compensation and benefits systems—in the same breath. On the benefits side, though, a growing number of responsible senior executives want to rethink their organization's involvement. Not only do they want to push the costs down (in immediate response to the raging increases in the cost of health care and the enforced discipline of the FAS accounting rule changes) but also to perhaps reengineer the entire effort to gain a longer-term, positive effect.

In that context, both in the long- and near-term views, what are some insurers doing to help meet the needs of our corporate benefits clients? In health insurance, some of us are moving aggressively into the managed care field. Others are maintaining the status quo, and the rest are getting out of this business.

Met and Managed Care

A decade ago, Met Life recognized our customers' frustration with rising medical costs, and we committed to converting Met Life from an indemnity health insurer to a managed care company. We knew then that to serve our customers in the future we would have to change from being a claims payer to being a health care cost manager, able to assist customers and their employees in the intelligent purchase of quality health care services.

Using health claims data and information technology, we set about selecting cost-effective, quality providers and contracting with them to form health care networks. This meant developing a spectrum of managed care services—from preferred provider organizations to HMOs (including point-of-service plans, multi-option plans, and tradition lock-in plans)—as well as all the related member services, provider relations, medical management, and quality assurance capability which improve managed care services. Indeed, we committed to becoming an HMO company in health care, which may ultimately have us operating group and/or staff model HMOs as well as our current Independent Practice Associations (IPA) models.

Since not all our customers are ready to commit to the most efficient models of health plans, we are offering a spectrum of health plans from traditional indemnity through the most efficient models of managed or "coordinated" care: the well-run HMO, organized medical groups, the accountable health partnership, and so on. Some of us are encouraging our customers to move more rapidly to the more efficient models by offering "try it, you'll like it" approaches, like point-of-service plans, to help organizations ease the transition to these models of health care delivery.

Reforming Without Government Control

Although most of America has still not accepted managed care, this is an effective track and is ultimately the only one leading to private sector control of costs while maintaining choice and quality in our national health system. Controlling health costs by direct government action through either a federal price control program or, at the extreme, adopting socialized medicine is definitely not the way to go. Although we cannot long continue to afford the traditional malfunctioning market of unfettered fee-for-service, government control would rob us of choice, erode our freedom, and surely drag down the quality of health care available to Americans. Managed care companies and some HMOs are ready to work with government to reform our national health system into one that provides the highest quality care in the world at an acceptable cost for every American.

It is well recognized that our health care system carries a very heavy administrative burden, a large part of which is caused by private health insurance systems. To address this, the industry has committed to dramatically expanding the use of technology to reduce costs. Both commercial carriers and the Blue Cross/Blue Shield organizations are committed to an electronic data interchange in the processing of at least 50 percent of all health care claim transactions over the next five years. As a major undertaking in cooperation with the Health Care Financing Administration, the interchange will not only involve movement in electronic technology, telecommunications and switching, but it will also establish further uniform data sets and formats. Most important, advancements in electronic claim adjudication capability on the part of insurers will be necessary in order to take full advantage of the electronic connectivity with the provider community.

The National Electronic Information Corporation, which already serves as an electronic transmission and clearinghouse switching facility for millions of medical claims each year, is in the process of establishing an on-line, interactive switching capability for managed care programs. This will address the need of commercial insurers, Blue Cross/Blue Shields, independent HMOs and any other health plan for eligibility, certification, benefit confirmation, and pre-authorization processing.

Insurance Companies Insure, Again

As still another way of meeting emerging client demands, the industry is more and more prepared to resume the role of insurer for health plans. Large numbers of employers in the 1970s and 1980s decided to enter the health insurance business. However, many are beginning to question the wisdom of that decision because the organizations had to establish themselves as the payer of last resort for health benefits, as well as becoming experts on benefit plan design, claims management, provider negotiation, and so forth. Insurers are ready and willing to resume their original role. Behavior changes will be needed: Many carriers will have to relearn how to successfully accept and manage risk, while employers will need to learn to transfer risk.

If employers are no longer insurers, what should be their role in employee benefits? We are moving toward employers defining in advance their dollar contribution to benefits and offering to employees an array of benefit products supplied by insurers and others; the price of these benefits would be reasonable, recognizing the purchasing power of the group. Employees retain choice with the advantages of volume discounts, of reduced distribution costs, and of the convenience of payroll deduction. This is a very different role from the traditional U.S. employee benefits picture of the past, but we are already moving along that path. Flexible benefit plans for active and retired employees are increasing. Employee-pay-all options for group auto, homeowners and long term care insurance are also increasing.

A final way some insurers, including Met Life, are serving the needs of their clients is through tasks of benefits administration that were formerly handled exclusively by benefits departments. We accept these assignments on a fee basis. The jobs can include dealing directly with employees on benefits matters; maintaining records; and interacting directly with payroll departments, carriers and other vendors on insurance as well as other benefits. Our customers have decided that we are more cost-effective than they are, and we can provide equally high quality of service.